RACIAL JUSTICE IN AMERICA

What Are MY RIGHTS?

We The People

KELISA WING

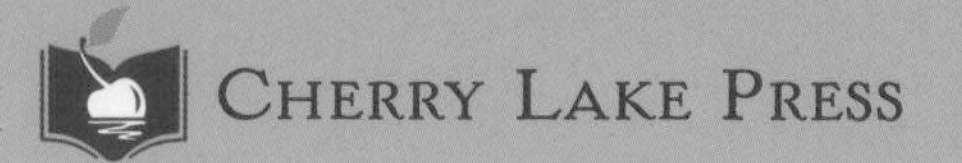

Published in the United States of America by Cherry Lake Publishing Group
Ann Arbor, Michigan
www.cherrylakepublishing.com

Reading Adviser: Marla Conn, MS, Ed., Literacy specialist, Read-Ability, Inc.
Content Adviser: Kelisa Wing
Book Design and Cover Art: Felicia Macheske

Photo Credits: © Rawpixel.com/Shutterstock.com, 6, 27; Library of Congress Control No.: 2003675329, 9; Library of Congress/Photograph by Warren K. Leffeler, LOC Control No.: 2014645538, 10; Library of Congress/Photograph by Marion S. Trikosko, LOC Control No.: 2013647403, 12; © Everett Collection/Shutterstock.com, 13; © Sundry Photography/Shutterstock.com, 14; © a katz/Shutterstock.com, 17; © VDB Photos/Shutterstock.com, 19; © Craig Chaddock/Shutterstock.com, 21; Library of Congress/Photograph by Dick DeMarsico, LOC Control No.: 99404328, 22; © Helder Almeida/Shutterstock.com, 25; © Joseph Sohm/Shutterstock.com, 30; © steve estvanik/Shutterstock.com, 31

Graphics Throughout: © debra hughes/Shutterstock.com; © GoodStudio/Shutterstock.com; © Natewimon Nantiwat/Shutterstock.com; © Galyna_P/Shutterstock.com

Library of Congress Cataloging-in-Publication Data

Names: Wing, Kelisa, author.
Title: What are my rights? / Kelisa Wing.
Description: Ann Arbor, Michigan : Cherry Lake Publishing, 2021. | Series: Racial justice in America | Includes index. | Audience: Grades 4-6 | Summary: "Race in America has been avoided in children's education for too long. What Are My Rights? explores the right you have in school, activism, and with the police in a comprehensive, honest, and age-appropriate way. Developed in conjunction with educator, advocate, and author Kelisa Wing to reach children of all races and encourage them to approach race issues with open eyes and minds. Includes 21st Century Skills and content, as well as a PBL activity across the Racial Justice in America series. Also includes a table of contents, glossary, index, author biography, sidebars, educational matter, and activities"— Provided by publisher.
Identifiers: LCCN 2020039991 (print) | LCCN 2020039992 (ebook) | ISBN 9781534180246 (hardcover) | ISBN 9781534181953 (paperback) | ISBN 9781534181250 (pdf) | ISBN 9781534182967 (ebook)
Subjects: LCSH: Civil rights—United States—Juvenile literature. | Social justice—United States—Juvenile literature. | United States—Race relations—Juvenile literature.
Classification: LCC JC599.U5 W56 2021 (print) | LCC JC599.U5 (ebook) | DDC 323.0973—dc23
LC record available at https://lccn.loc.gov/2020039991
LC ebook record available at https://lccn.loc.gov/2020039992

Cherry Lake Publishing Group would like to acknowledge the work of the Partnership for 21st Century Learning, a Network of Battelle for Kids. Please visit *http://www.battelleforkids.org/networks/p21* for more information.

Printed in the United States of America
Corporate Graphics

For Naima and Jadon

Kelisa Wing honorably served in the U.S. Army and has been an educator for 14 years. She is the author of *Promises and Possibilities: Dismantling the School to Prison Pipeline*, *If I Could: Lessons for Navigating an Unjust World*, and *Weeds & Seeds: How to Stay Positive in the Midst of Life's Storms*. She speaks both nationally and internationally about discipline reform, equity, and student engagement. Kelisa lives in Northern Virginia with her husband and two children.

Chapter 1
Introduction to Your Rights | Page 4

Chapter 2
History of Rights in America | Page 8

Chapter 3
Current Action | Page 16

DO THE WORK! | Page 24

Chapter 4
How to Be Anti-Racist and an Ally for Rights | Page 26

Extend Your Learning | Page 32

Glossary | Page 32

Index | Page 32

CHAPTER 1

Introduction to Your Rights

You may have heard that you have the right to "life, liberty, and the pursuit of happiness." This phrase comes from the Declaration of Independence, a document created in 1776 by our nation's Founding Fathers. The rights promised in this document are **inalienable**. The Bill of Rights, the first 10 amendments of the U.S. Constitution, gives Americans additional rights, including the rights to freedom of speech, press, and **assembly**.

These freedoms are promised to our citizens through documents created at our nation's birth. All people are legally, morally, and socially entitled to them.

IN CONGRESS, JULY 4, 1776.

The unanimous Declaration of the thirteen united States of America,

Fifty-six men signed the Declaration of Independence. John Hancock's signature was the most prominent.

While it's important to have documents that establish rights, it's equally important to have rules in place to protect those rights. Over the years, we have passed laws to **prohibit discrimination** on the basis of race, age, **gender**, and ability. However, some would say we still have a long way to go.

Discrimination is a violation of our inalienable rights.

What does all of this mean for you as a student? It means you have a right to speak your mind in school, a right to express yourself through speech, and a right to a free public education. You have these rights no matter what your race, religion, gender, or national origin is.

Your rights matter. Understanding your rights will help you as a student and as you continue to learn and grow.

Critical Thinking

Did you know that rules in your school cannot interfere with the rights you have? What are the rules in your school? What would you do to speak up and speak out against rules that violate your rights? For example, does your dress code go against your rights? Are there rules that target girls or boys specifically?

CHAPTER 2

History of Rights in America

Today, many people are concerned about their rights when it comes to equal treatment, voting, protest, and free speech. We understand that we all have rights, but how did they come to be? Let's look at the history of some of the movements that gave us those rights and paved the way for the protests of today.

In 1848, a group of **activists** in Seneca Falls, New York, gathered to discuss fighting for the right of women to vote. At the time, only White men could vote. This meeting was called the Seneca Falls Convention. In 1869, Susan B. Anthony and Elizabeth Cady Stanton founded the National Woman Suffrage Association to fight for an amendment to the U.S. Constitution that would give women the vote. The group merged with a second group in 1890 and became the National American Woman Suffrage Association. It took many years of fighting for their rights, but in 1920, the 19th Amendment was added to the Constitution. Women could now vote in all elections.

The women's suffrage movement worked for more than 70 years before achieving their goal.

For Black people in America, it took much longer to gain true rights of equality. The 15th Amendment had granted Black men the right to vote in 1870. But Jim Crow laws had already begun. These **racist** laws forced Black people to drink from separate water fountains, attend **segregated** schools, and use separate restrooms. In addition, these laws were taking away the rights promised by the 15th Amendment.

Jim Crow laws made it difficult for Black people to vote in national and local elections—and were a violation of rights.

Events of the 1950s and 1960s caused the calls for **civil rights** to grow louder. Emmett Till, a Black 14-year-old, was brutally murdered in Mississippi for supposedly flirting with a White woman. Rosa Parks refused to give up her seat on an Alabama bus to a White man. And the Black students who became the Little Rock Nine bravely tried to attend a White high school in Arkansas. After years of protests, marches, and demonstrations, the Civil Rights Act of 1964 was finally signed into law. This outlawed discrimination and enforced desegregation. The next year, the Voting Rights Act of 1965 became law, giving Black people equal voting rights and protections from racist voting rules.

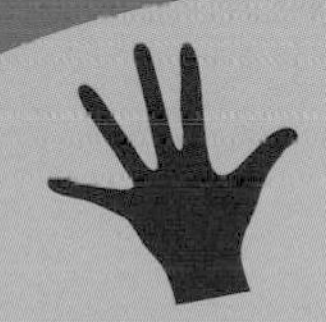

Take a virtual tour of the National Museum of African American History and Culture by visiting *https://nmaahc.si.edu*. There are 35,000 artifacts that tell the story of Black people in America. After visiting, think about what else you learned about the history of rights.

The March on Washington

Have you ever felt helpless? What did you do in that moment? Did you quit or keep going? During the civil rights era, people who felt helpless not only kept going, but they also marched! The March on Washington was held on the National Mall in 1963 and drew over 250,000 people. Congressman John Lewis was the youngest person to speak at the march. He was just 23! He was the last living speaker from that day until he died on July 17, 2020. What other facts can you find out about John Lewis and the March on Washington?

Martin Luther King Jr. delivered his famous “I Have a Dream” speech at the March on Washington.

What is gerrymandering? Look online to find out. How does gerrymandering interfere with fair elections?

The legal rights that let all Americans vote safely and expect equal education and treatment under the law were the result of activists who were willing to speak up and speak out for what is right and fair. And their fight isn't over. Civil rights and voting rights are always under attack. Discrimination is still a problem.

Talk to a teacher about where they still see unfairness under the law. Think about the rights and treatment of Black people, members of the LGBTQ communities, and women.

CHAPTER 3

Current Action

Many people are still fighting for what is right and fair today. Protesting is one of the best ways to get your voice heard. And the right to protest is protected by the U.S. Constitution. There are two reasons why people protest.

One reason is because people feel strongly about something. An example is when student activists organized March for Our Lives in March 2018 following the mass shooting at Marjory Stoneman Douglas High School. The protest was the largest against gun violence in history. The students turned this single event into an organization that would help people get registered to vote, learn about their rights, and end gun violence. Another example of people protesting for or against something they feel strongly about is climate change. People are fighting for climate change by promising to recycle, carpool, call their government officials, and buy things that are better for the environment.

In 2014, more than 300,000 people marched in New York City's People's Climate March.

People also protest to fight for their rights or the rights of others. The Black Lives Matter movement (BLM) is an example of this type of protest. BLM began in 2013 in response to the mistreatment of Black people and the murder of Trayvon Martin. Today, the movement is dedicated to the freedom of Black people to live without racism.

After the murder of George Floyd in Minneapolis in May 2020, there were BLM protests in over 2,000 cities and 60 countries. Protesters called for racial justice and demanded an end to the mistreatment of people of color in America. The protests in 2020 were the largest in U.S. history.

Do you ever think you are too young to be heard? It is important for you to know that you have rights and you are never too young to make a difference! Eight-year-old Nolan Davis realized this when in June 2020 he organized a Children's Black Lives Matter March in Minnesota. In what ways can you use your voice to make a difference?

"Injustice anywhere is a threat to justice everywhere" means that even if a particular injustice doesn't directly effect you, the fact that it exists puts you and your rights at risk.

Another example of protesting to work for the rights of others is the fight in 2020 for equal voting rights. Congressman John Lewis worked tirelessly for voting rights his whole life. After he died in July 2020, people asked the U.S. Congress to address problems involving **mail-in voting**, **absentee voting**, and **voter suppression**.

What other issues do you see people in your community protesting against?

Life as a Reporter

Learning about the backgrounds of others is the best way to eliminate racism. Find a friend in class who has a different background than you. Research their nationality, race, and traditions by interviewing them. Understanding more about the people around us allows us to see that we are all, as Martin Luther King Jr. said, "human and therefore brothers."

John Lewis served in the U.S. House of Representatives for more than 30 years.

Martin Luther King Jr. was known for his organization of nonviolent protests against segregation and voting inequalities.

Did You Know?

An activist is a person who campaigns to bring about political or social change. Martin Luther King Jr. said, "Life's most persistent and urgent question is: 'What are you doing for others?'" Think about something you have done to make a difference for other people. How can you be more of an activist for your rights and the rights of others? Take a pledge to stand up and speak out about injustices for yourself and for others. By taking a stand, you can serve others and make the world a better place.

Did you know we have the right to protest? This is a right guaranteed by the First Amendment of the Constitution. If this is true, why have so many people been arrested for protesting? There are several reasons. They can be arrested if they are:

- vandalizing property, buildings, or statues
- trespassing or blocking entryways of buildings
- blocking traffic
- breaking a curfew that has been put in place by law
- refusing to **disperse**
- taking part in violence or property destruction

We can protest, but we must do so peacefully.

DO THE WORK!

ESSENTIAL QUESTION

How can we be anti-racist?

Becoming anti-racist requires actively working against racism using words and actions. This project-based learning assignment will allow you to practice these skills. Read all the books in the *Racial Justice in America* series. Through each "DO THE WORK!" activity, you will research and put together parts of a larger project that will allow you to grow and help others grow as well.

So far, you have learned about your rights and what people have done in the past—and are doing today—to fight for those rights. How does learning about the past

help us to understand our future? Research the civil rights movement and the current movement for racial justice. Choose one right that deals with racial justice from the past. Compare and contrast it to the rights that are currently being fought for today. Find a creative way to show the differences and similarities. How would you create racial justice?

For the presentation of your final work, you can create a collage, magazine, podcast, jigsaw puzzle, poem, video, or social media campaign—anything to demonstrate your learning. No matter what you do, just be creative, learn something new, and publicize your work!

CHAPTER 4

How to Be Anti-Racist and an Ally for Rights

Now you know that you have the right to assemble peacefully with others and speak out about what is important to you. We must ensure we uphold rights for ourselves and others—especially those inalienable rights. Calling for social and racial justice is a key part of being an anti-racist activist and an **ally**. Beyond just protesting, there are many ways to do this. You can speak up, out, and against injustices you see in your everyday life. You can face everyday **bias** head-on.

Being an activist for equal rights and ally for marginalized communities is hard work.

Be an ADVOCATE!

Advocating for rights takes courage. There will be many situations where you will have to decide whether to be a **bystander** or an ally. You can be **empowered** to speak up by using these techniques:

1. **QUESTION:** Ask the person who is violating other people's rights, "Why are you treating others that way?"

2. **CHALLENGE:** Ask them, "Why do you think this way?"

3. **CORRECT:** Tell them the truth by saying, "That is not true. The truth is, no one is less than anyone and we all have the right to life, liberty, and equity."

This can be scary, because we wonder what our friends will think about us if we say something. But we have to speak up and out against racism.

Be ready to confront bias and racism when it happens. Use the questions on these pages to help you stand up against injustice. We can also educate our friends about our differences at the moment a bias occurs. These situations will not only happen in school. They can also occur in the store, in our homes—everywhere in our communities. We have to be an ally and an anti-racist in all situations and places.

You have the power to make a difference in this world by knowing your rights, speaking up and out, protesting when necessary, and facing bias head-on.

One Person Can Make a Difference

1. In 1989, a man in China stood in the street and blocked military tanks from intimidating others.

2. Rosa Parks refused to give up her seat on a bus to a White man in 1955, leading to a nationwide bus **boycott**.

3. Mahatma Gandhi would often use **hunger strikes** as a way to protest injustices throughout India.

4. In the summer of 2020, there were one-person BLM protests in Louisiana, Wisconsin, Minnesota, Illinois, North Carolina, Washington, California, Oregon, Virginia, Florida, Texas, Nebraska, Arkansas, and Tennessee.

Rosa Parks's one-woman protest sparked the fire that changed America's segregation laws.

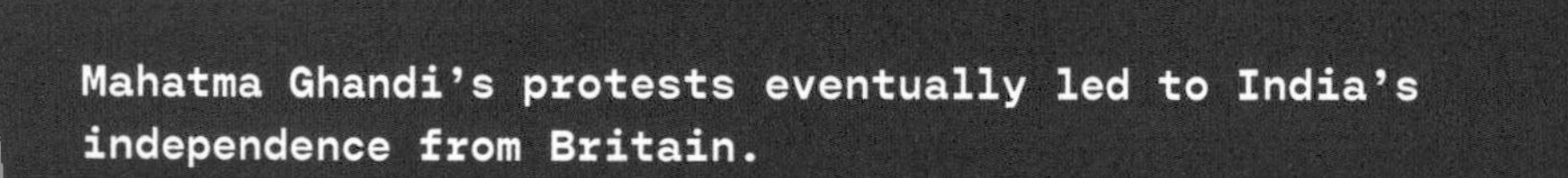

Mahatma Ghandi's protests eventually led to India's independence from Britain.

EXTEND YOUR LEARNING

Bridges, Ruby. *Through My Eyes*. New York, NY: Scholastic, 1999.

Lewis, John. *March: Book One*. Marietta, GA: Top Shelf Productions, 2013.

National Center for Civil and Human Rights
https://www.civilandhumanrights.org/about-us

Smithsonian National Museum of African American History and Culture
https://nmaahc.si.edu

Thomsen, Ian. "How Do Today's Black Lives Matter Protests Compare to the Civil Rights Movement of the 1960s?" News@ Northeastern University, June 4, 2020. *https://news.northeastern.edu/2020/06/04/how-do-todays-black-lives-matter-protests-compare-to-the-civil-rights-movement-of-the-1960s.*

GLOSSARY

absentee voting (ab-suhn-TEE VOHT-ing) casting a vote in advance of an election by mail, by someone who cannot vote in person and requested a ballot ahead of time

activists (AK-tuh-vists) people who fight to bring about political or social change

ally (AL-eye) a person who is on the same side as another during a disagreement; a supporter

assembly (uh-SEM-blee) gathering together in one place of a lot of people for a common purpose

bias (BYE-uhs) a personal judgment in favor of or against a thing, person, or group, usually in a way considered to be unfair

boycott (BOI-kot) to refuse to buy or use something as a punishment or protest

bystander (BYE-stan-dur) a person who is present at an event or incident but does not take part

civil rights (SIV-uhl RITES) the rights everyone should have to freedom and equal treatment under the law, regardless of who they are

discrimination (dis-krim-uh-NAY-shuhn) the unfair treatment of others based on differences in such things as race, age, or gender

disperse (dis-PURS) to scatter or move in different directions

empowered (im-POU-urd) having the ability to act thanks to knowledge or skills

gender (JEN-dur) the male or female sex

hunger strikes (HUNG-ger STRIKES) prolonged refusals to eat, carried out as a protest often by prisoners

inalienable (in-AY-lee-uhn-nuh-buhl) unable to be taken away from or given away by someone

mail-in voting (MAYL-in VOHT-ing) voting that is done by all citizens of certain states; they receive their ballots by mail and return them that way or drop them off at ballot boxes

prohibit (proh-HIB-it) to forbid or ban something by law, rule, or other authority

racist (RAY-sist) a person who treats people unfairly or cruelly because of their race

segregated (SEG-rih-gate-id) separated or kept apart in a place, such as Blacks separated from Whites

voter suppression (VOHT-ur suh-PRESH-uhn) a strategy used to influence the outcome of an election by discouraging or preventing specific groups of people from voting

INDEX

activists/activism, 8, 11, 15, 16–17, 23, 26–31
Anthony, Susan B., 8–9
anti-racism
  activity, 24–25
  how to advocate for, 26–31

bias, racial, 26, 29
Black Lives Matter, 18, 30

civil rights, 11, 12, 15
Civil Rights Act of 1964, 11
climate change, 17

Declaration of Independence, 4–5
demonstrations, 11
desegregation, 11
discrimination, 6, 11, 15
"Do the Work!" activity, 24–25

education, equal, 15
elections, 14. See also voting
equality, 10–11

15th Amendment, 10
Floyd, George, 18
freedoms, 4

Gandhi, Mahatma, 30, 31
gerrymandering, 14
gun violence, 16

"I Have a Dream" speech, 13
inequalities, 22
injustice, 19, 23, 26, 29

Jim Crow laws, 10
justice, racial, 18, 19, 26, 30

King, Martin Luther Jr., 13, 20, 22, 23

laws, 6, 10, 30
Lewis, John, 12, 20, 21
Little Rock Nine, 11

March for Our Lives, 16
March on Washington, 12–13
marches, 11, 12–13, 16–17
Martin, Trayvon, 18
mass shootings, 16

National Woman Suffrage Association, 8
19th Amendment, 8–9

Parks, Rosa, 11, 30
People's Climate March, 17
protests, 11, 16–23, 26, 30–31

racism, 10, 20
rights
  current action, 16–23
  history of, in America, 8–15
  how one person can make a difference, 30–31
  how to be an ally for, 26–31
  introduction to, 4–7
rules, 6, 7

segregation, 10, 11, 22
social justice, 26
Stanton, Elizabeth Cady, 8

Till, Emmett, 11

voting, 8–9, 10, 11, 15, 20, 22
Voting Rights Act of 1965, 11

women's rights, 8–9